PREHISTORIC LIFE

THE
AGE OF MAMMALS

RUPERT MATTHEWS

Artist: Carolyn Scrace

The Bookwright Press
New York • 1990

Titles in this series

How Life Began
The Dinosaur Age
The Age of Mammals

Ice Age Animals
The First People
The First Settlements

Cover illustration: A smilodon, with an
imperial mammoth in the background.

First published in the United States in 1990 by
The Bookwright Press
387 Park Avenue South
New York NY 10016

First published in 1989 by
Wayland (Publishers) Ltd
61 Western Road, Hove
East Sussex BN3 1JD, England

Library of Congress Cataloging-in-Publication Data
Matthews, Rupert.
    The age of mammals / by Rupert Matthews.
        p.   cm. – (Prehistoric life)
    Bibliography: p.
    Includes index.
    Summary: A survey of the characteristics and
natural environment of the earliest, now extinct,
mammals which are the ancestors of the modern
horses, elephants, cats, dogs, and primates.
    ISBN 0–531–18311–4
    1. Mammals, Fossil – Juvenile literature.
(1. Mammals, Fossil.) I. Title.   II. Series: Matthews, Rupert.
Prehistoric life.
QE881.M438   1990
569 – dc20   89-9800
                                                  CIP
                                                  AC

Typeset by Direct Image Photosetting Limited,
Hove, Sussex, England.
Printed by G. Canale and C.S.p.A., Turin, Italy

Contents

Words printed in **bold** are explained in the glossary.

The First Mammals

Most of the large animals on earth today are **mammals**. Elephants, lions, kangaroos and even humans are all mammals. There are also many small mammals such as rabbits, prairie dogs and mice.

Although there are many kinds of mammals, they all have certain features that make them different from other animals. The most noticeable of these is that most mammals are covered with fur. Even those mammals that do not have thick fur, such as humans and rhinoceroses, have some hair on their bodies. Mammals also have the ability to create their own body heat. This is known as being warm-blooded. Other creatures, such as **reptiles**, are cold-blooded, which means that they rely on their surroundings for heat. Birds are the only other creatures that are warm-blooded.

Mammals feed their young on milk. This provides the young with a supply of easily digested food. The milk is produced in mammary glands, which is where the word "mammal" comes from.

The very first mammals were tiny creatures, only a few inches long. **Fossils** of these animals are very rare, so scientists do not know very much about them. However, it seems that the earliest mammals lived about 200 million years ago,

Modern mammals come in many different shapes and sizes. The largest land mammal is the African elephant (above). The dormouse (left) is one of the smallest.

soon after the first **dinosaurs**. For many millions of years mammals lived alongside the dinosaurs. These mammals probably became active only at night. Perhaps they hunted insects and worms.

Special teeth

Unlike other animals, mammals have teeth of several shapes. In a human jaw the back teeth are wide and flat. In front of these are sharp teeth which are slightly longer. At the very front are narrow teeth used for biting. Other animals do not have these differences. The teeth of a reptile, for instance, are all the same shape, although they differ in size.

Below: **The Delta-theridium was one of the earliest mammals. It lived about 70 million years ago, at the same time as the giant dinosaurs.**

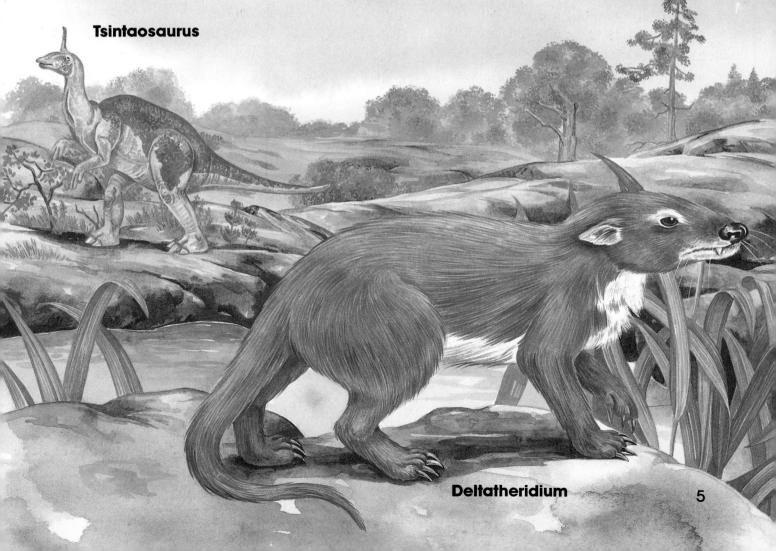

Tsintaosaurus

Deltatheridium

The End of the Dinosaurs

About 65 million years ago the animal life of the earth changed suddenly. Many types of animals died out. Nobody knows exactly why this happened. Perhaps the **climate** changed or food suddenly became scarce. Whatever the cause, all the large reptiles eventually became **extinct**. This included all the dinosaurs and flying reptiles.

Only a few types of animals survived, but these animals were now able to **evolve**. They were no longer hunted by the large reptiles and it was easier for them to find food. The mammals took advantage of these opportunities.

Three main types of mammals had already appeared during the time of the dinosaurs. These were the **placentals**, the **marsupials** and the **prototherians**.

The prototherians were the most common at the time, and there were many different kinds. Today only two types of prototherian survive: the platypus and the spiny anteater.

The marsupials were less common. They gave birth when the young were very small. The young stayed in a pouch of their mother's skin until they were old enough to survive on their own. Kangaroos are a type of modern

Below: **Plesiadapis was one of the earliest mammals.**

Plesiadapis

marsupial.

Placental mammals gave birth to young that were fully formed and did not need to stay in a pouch. Humans are placental mammals.

Very few fossils of early mammals have been found but scientists believe that these creatures did not change much for several million years. They were very similar to the animals that had lived at the time of the dinosaurs but they included the earliest members of important groups such as the **primates** and **ungulates**, which we will look at later in this book.

Right: **The spiny anteater of Australia, a living prototherian.**

Survivors and casualties

About 65 million years ago, many types of animals became extinct. Other groups survived unharmed. Among the animals that vanished were the dinosaurs, **plesiosaurs**, **pterodactyls** and smaller animals such as **ammonites** and microscopic **plankton**. Creatures that survived included mammals, birds, some reptiles, lizards and fish. Nobody knows why some lived and others died.

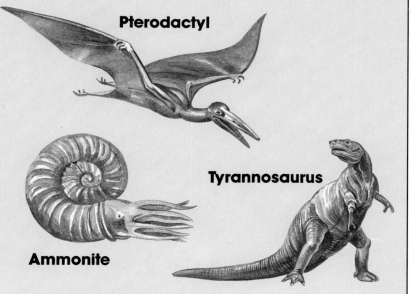

Pterodactyl

Tyrannosaurus

Ammonite

The Mammals Develop

As the mammals evolved, they developed into many new forms. Some mammals became adapted to eating plants, others to eating animals. Many mammals became much larger.

However, the mammals were not the only creatures taking advantage of the disappearance of the dinosaurs. The birds also evolved rapidly. In North America, a family of hunting birds called diatrymas appeared. These birds could not fly, but were able to run extremely quickly. With their speed and power the diatrymas were able to catch and eat prey. The largest of these birds stood over 2 m (6.5 ft) tall.

Two groups of plant-eating mammals became important: the pantodonts and the condylarths. One of the largest pantodonts was *Barylambda*. This bulky creature was about the size of a cow and had strong, heavy legs. About 50 million years ago a 3 m (10 ft) long pantodont called *Coryphodon* lived in swamps and lakes. It is thought that this animal behaved like a modern hippopotamus, spending most of its time in the water. The water helped to support the heavy weight of its large body. This meant that *Coryphodon* was able to move around more easily.

Below: **The Diatryma was a large, meat-eating bird which hunted early types of mammals.**

Diatryma

Coryphodon

The second group of plant-eating mammals was the condylarths. These creatures are the ancestors of most modern plant-eating mammals. *Phenacodus*, which lived in North America 54 million years ago, was about the same size as a sheep, but had a long tail. It walked on the soles of its feet, and had toes that splayed outward and ended with small hoofs. Its teeth were large and flat, which made them suited to grinding up plants. *Phenacodus* probably lived in forests and ate leaves from trees and shrubs.

The remains of the earliest known bat are about the same age as the fossils of *Phenacodus*. These remains were found in Wyoming. The creature is called *Icaronycteris*, and was only a few inches long. It was similar to modern bats and was able to fly very well. Scientists think that the first true bats appeared several million years earlier, but they have not found any fossils to prove this.

Above: **Coryphodon lived in swamps, but may have climbed onto dry land to look for plants to eat.**

Early Hunters

While some mammals were evolving into plant-eating animals, others became meat eaters. These creatures developed different physical features to suit the way they lived. Meat eaters need sharp teeth and claws to kill their prey. They must also be able to catch other animals, so they can usually run quickly; or they have good **camouflage** to help them to hide while waiting to catch their prey.

The earliest meat-eating mammals are known as creodonts. These animals were rather similar to plant eaters such as *Phenacodus*. About 54 million years ago, *Oxyaena* lived in North America. This creature was about 1 m (3 ft) long and probably hunted small mammals and perhaps reptiles. It had a large skull with strong jaws and sharp teeth.

Some creodonts were similar to dogs. They could run quickly and probably chased their prey. Some scientists think that animals such as *Dromocyon* hunted in packs.

Right:
Creodonts had sharp teeth and claws which they used to kill other animals.

Dromocyon

Though they were the most important meat eaters for millions of years, the creodonts eventually died out. Nobody knows why. One of the last was a creature called *Hyaenodon*, which lived about 34 million years ago. This creature was about the size of a large dog, but looked more like a hyena. Scientists think that it may have lived by eating the meat of animals killed by other hunters.

The ancestors of modern cats and dogs were not creodonts, but small creatures known as miacids. The miacids were originally hunters that scampered through the forests feeding on animals smaller than themselves. For several million years they were not very common, but about 38 million years ago they replaced the creodonts as the most important meat eaters.

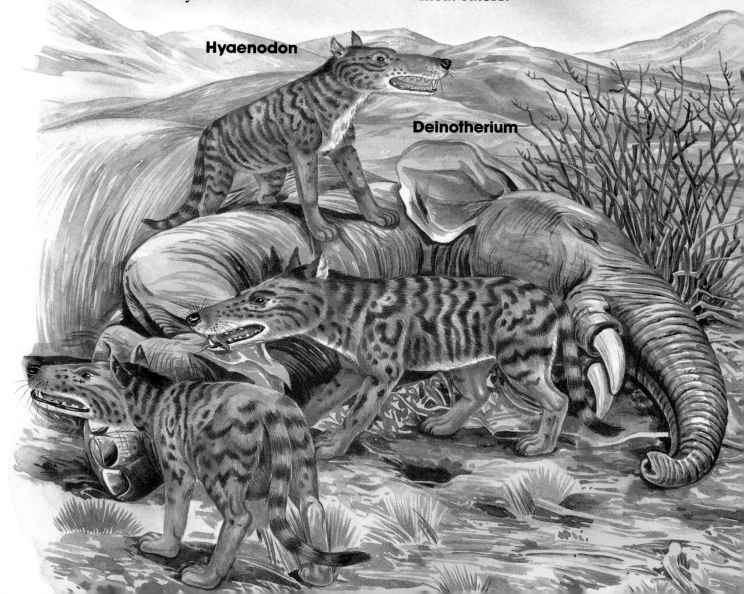

Hyaenodon

Deinotherium

The Horses

Scientists depend upon fossils for their knowledge of prehistoric animals. But very few animals become fossilized, and scientists are hardly ever able to find out how an animal evolved from the very beginning to the present day. However, the evolution of the horse is almost fully known.

Horses are probably descended from condylarths such as *Phenacodus*. The earliest animal that is known to be a member of the horse family is *Hyracotherium*. This animal lived in Europe and North America about 50 million years ago. It was much smaller than modern horses, standing only 45 cm (18 in) tall. *Hyracotherium* lived in forests and ate leaves and shoots. Like its condylarth ancestors, this horse had several toes on each foot, four at the front and three at the rear. Modern horses have one toe in the form of a hoof.

As time passed, the descendants of *Hyracotherium* became larger, but otherwise changed little. *Mesohippus*, for instance, stood 70 cm (27 in) tall, but it still lived in forests and had several toes. The development of the modern horse came about because of a change in climate. About 20 million years ago the climate of the world gradually became drier. The lack of rain caused the disappearance of many forests. Grasslands formed in their place. Animals, including the horses, had to adapt to these new conditions.

By 18 million years ago a new type of horse, *Merychippus*, had appeared. This animal stood over 1 m (3 ft) high and had habits similar to modern horses'. It lived on open grassland and was able to run very

Hyracotherium

quickly. It had three toes on each foot, but only one reached the ground to form a hoof. The teeth were tough and specially shaped to allow *Merychippus* to grind up tough grass stems more easily.

At about the same time, several other types of horse appeared which were similar to *Merychippus*. These became taller and faster as they developed. The true modern horse, known scientifically as *Equus*, appeared about two million years ago in America. It then spread to Asia and Europe. Strangely, the horse died out in America, perhaps through disease, but it became common in Asia and Europe, where it has survived to the present day.

Below: Horses became larger and faster as they adapted to life on open grasslands.

Merychippus

Equus

Weird Rhinoceroses

Most people know what a present-day rhinoceros looks like. They have probably seen one on television, or seen a picture in a book. Though there are several types of rhinoceros alive today, they all share certain features. They are all fairly large, being 1-2 m (3-6 ft) tall and 2-4 m (6-13 ft) long. Rhinoceroses are heavy, powerful plant eaters. They have one or two sharp horns, which they use to drive off **predators**. This form is a recent development in the rhinoceros family.

Like horses, rhinoceroses are descended from condylarths. One of the earliest rhinoceroses was called *Metamyndon*. This creature lived in America and Asia about 35 million years ago. It was over 4 m (13 ft) long and looked rather like a small hippopotamus. Scientists think that it lived in swamps, eating water plants and rarely moving on to dry land. These water rhinoceroses survived for several million years but eventually died out.

**Below right:
The biggest land mammal of all time was the Indrico-therium of India.**

Hyracodon

**Right:
Hyracodon lived on open plains and needed to be able to run fast to escape from predators or, as here, from fire.**

The modern rhino

The ancestors of modern rhinoceroses lived about 42 million years ago. These creatures did not develop horns until about 30 million years ago. Once, there were many rhinoceroses but they have recently declined in number. Only a few species survive and all of these are in danger of extinction.

Indricotherium

A few million years later a new type of running rhinoceros, called *Hyracodon*, became common in North America. This small animal was adapted to life in the grasslands. Like early horses, this creature was adapted to run on its toes. All animals that need to run fast use only their toes.

The most amazing of the early rhinoceroses were the huge indricotheres, which lived in Asia about 30 million years ago. The biggest, *Indricotherium*, stood 6 m (19.6 ft) at the shoulder and weighed over 14 tons. It was the largest land mammal ever – twice as large as a modern elephant. These creatures died out when elephants reached Asia. Perhaps the elephants ate the same food and robbed the indricotheres of supplies.

Ancient Elephants

Platybelodon

Like the rhinoceros family, the elephant family is much smaller today than it once was. Only two types of elephants are alive today, the African and the Indian. Both of these creatures have long tusks and a trunk. The African elephant has very large ears. Some prehistoric elephants shared these features, but others were very different.

The earliest-known member of the elephant family was *Moeritherium* which lived 45 million years ago in North Africa. This creature did not look very much like an elephant. It was only about 70 cm (27 in) tall and had short, stumpy legs. The head was long and low, without trunk, tusks or large ears. *Moeritherium* probably lived in swamps or rivers, and may have eaten water plants.

Within ten million years, the elephants had divided into two families, four-tuskers and two-tuskers. The four-tusker elephants had tusks in both upper and lower jaws. One of these creatures is known as *Platybelodon*, the "shovel elephant." The lower jaw of *Platybelodon* was very long and wide. It ended in two shovel-shaped teeth with which the animal rooted up plants. The trunk was short and was probably used to move food from the "shovel" to the

Above: **Platybelodon was a very unusual elephant with teeth specially adapted to digging up swamp plants.**

16

back of the mouth. *Platybelodon* lived in Mongolia and North America about eight million years ago.

There were also several different types of two-tusker elephantine animals. The most unusual of these were the deinotheres. These animals had tusks in their lower jaws which pointed downward. Nobody is quite sure why these tusks developed, but possibly they were used for digging up roots. The largest of these was *Deinotherium* which stood 4 m (13 ft) tall and lived about three million years ago in Europe.

Mastodons were two-tusked relatives of elephants whose teeth were shaped differently from those of true elephants. The first mastodons lived in Egypt about 38 million years ago. Some migrated to America where they survived until about 10,000 years ago. The mammoths originated some two million years ago. They produced many different species before the famous woolly mammoth appeared during the Ice Ages. Eventually these different animals died out, leaving only the two modern elephant species.

Below: **Nobody is certain why Deinotherium had tusks that pointed downward. Perhaps they were used for finding food or in fights between rivals.**

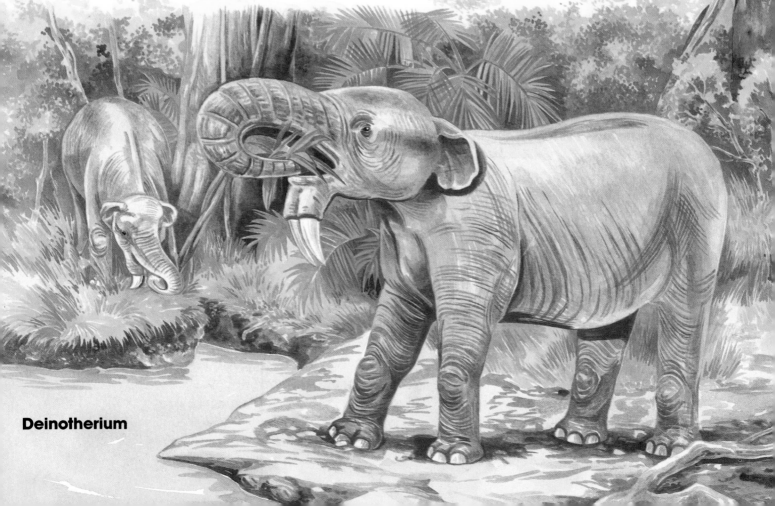

Deinotherium

Beasts with Cloven Hoofs

Right: **Aepycamelus ate leaves from tree branches in North America.**

About 55 million years ago the first members of a very important group of mammals appeared. These were the even-toed ungulates, which include all plant eaters with an even number of hoofs, such as cattle, deer and camels. At first these creatures were small and fast-running. They lived in both America and Europe.

One branch of the even-toed ungulates is known as the suiforms. Several different members of this family appeared and about 32 million years ago they developed into the pigs. Several species of wild pig survived in Europe and Africa.

The second branch of even-toed ungulates developed a special method of feeding, known as rumination. This involves two separate stages of eating. First, plants are bitten off and swallowed into the **rumen**. Here they remain until the animal **regurgitates** them. The plant food is then thoroughly chewed and swallowed again. This time the food passes into the intestine and is digested. One major advantage of rumination is that the animal spends only a short time feeding in the open. It can then hide from predators while it chews its food.

Several different families of ruminants evolved. The camels first appeared in North America about 35 million years ago and developed into different forms. *Aepycamelus* lived about ten million years ago. It looked rather like a

Head ornaments

Many species of prehistoric ruminants had horns or antlers on their heads. These may have been weapons for fighting off predators, or for fights with rivals of the same species.

Ilingocerus

Ramocerus

Hayocerus

Aepycamelus

giraffe with its long neck, which helped it to reach leaves on high tree branches. Camels later became extinct in America, but species specially adapted to desert life survive in Africa and Asia.

The ancestor of both deer and giraffes appeared in Asia 40 million years ago. True deer did not evolve until about ten million years ago when *Dicrocerus* lived in Europe. This creature had small antlers with only two points. Later, deer grew bigger and their antlers became larger too.

The most advanced ruminants are the bovids, which include cattle, sheep, antelopes and goats. The first bovids evolved about 12 million years ago and rapidly spread throughout Africa, Europe, North America and Asia.

Giant Plant Eaters

Throughout the age of mammals some plant eaters grew to be much larger than other animals living at the same time. Some had strange-looking horns and spikes on their heads. These creatures were not related to each other. In some instances, scientists are not sure to which family they belong.

One of the first of these giant plant eaters was *Uintatherium*, which lived in North America about 42 million years ago. *Uintatherium* was nearly 4 m (13 ft) long and 2 m (6.5 ft) tall. It was a heavy animal and could not run fast. The remarkable head of this animal was topped by six bony lumps. Scientists are not sure what these odd-looking growths were for. A long line of similar, but smaller animals lived before *Uintatherium*, but none after it. Nobody knows why they died out.

Below: Uintatherium was a massive, clumsy plant eater.

Uintatherium

Brontotherium

Ten million years later another lumbering giant lived in North America. This was the *Brontotherium*. It was a massive animal, with a muscular body and thick legs. Its nose was topped by an enormous bone which grew upward and divided in two. This strange growth may have been used in display or fights between rival *Brontotheria*. It is thought that these creatures fed on the plants that grew alongside the many lakes and marshes of the time. When these dried up the *Brontotheria* were starved of their food and died out.

Arsinoitherium lived in North Africa about 32 million years ago. Only one other species similar to this creature is thought to have existed. *Arsinoitherium* was over 3 m (10 ft) long and was very heavy. Its wide feet were designed to spread the weight of the animal over a wide area. This may mean that it walked on soft ground, such as swamps or marshes, or in forests on the edge of rivers. The huge horns that grew from its head were probably used as a defense against attackers.

Above: **Brontotherium's strange horn-like growth may have been used in fights with other giant plant eaters.**

21

The Cats

After the disappearance of the creodonts, two groups of mammals, the cats and the dogs, became the most important meat eaters. The earliest members of the cat family were small and short-legged, rather like modern civets and mongooses.

By about 35 million years ago creatures like modern cats had evolved. One of the earliest of these was *Dinictis,* which lived in North America. It was just over 1 m (3 ft) long and had long, sharp teeth with which to kill its prey. Like most modern cats, *Dinictis* probably hunted quietly. It would creep up on its victim and only at the last moment would it leap forward to attack the unfortunate plant eater.

After *Dinictis,* the cat family divided into several groups. One group is known as the stabbing cats. They had long, sharp teeth with which they attacked their victims. It is thought that they may have hunted large animals such as horses, elephants and rhinoceroses. One of the largest and most powerful of these hunters was *Machairodus,* which lived in Europe about five million years ago. The stabbing teeth of this animal were nearly 20 cm (8 in) long. Its mouth was specially adapted to open enough to allow the teeth to be used. Although different types of stabbing cat evolved, the whole group eventually became extinct.

Another group of the cat family is known as the biting cats. All modern cats belong to this group, which hunts in a quite different way from the stabbing cats. The biting cats kill their prey by biting at the throat, rather than by stabbing through tough skin. Modern types of biting cat first appeared about seven million years ago.

Below: **Dinictis, one of the earliest members of the cat family, may have hunted by sneaking up on its victim and then pouncing.**

The silent hunter

Cats hunt very quietly. They creep up on their prey on padded feet. When they are close enough to spring, they rush forward and attack their prey with sharp claws. The tiger, which lives throughout much of Asia, is one of the largest cats. It measures 4 m (13 ft) long.

Dinictis

The Dogs

The dogs appeared at about the same time as the first cats. One of the earliest dogs was *Pseudocynodictis*, which lived about 35 million years ago in North America. This creature was similar to a modern weasel, with its short legs and long body. It was 1.5 m (5 ft) long.

About 35 million years ago the dog family divided into several different groups. One group changed very little and eventually became the modern otters and badgers. A second group became adapted to climbing trees. Today this group is represented by the racoons. Two other groups took to life in the water, and they became seals and sea lions.

Two other groups that developed from the dog family were the bears and the true dogs. The earliest bears were fairly small creatures and they lived about 20 million years ago in Europe. Within ten million years, they had evolved into much larger forms that were very similar to modern bears.

Pseudocynodictis

Mesohippus

The true dogs evolved first in Europe some 22 million years ago. They were highly successful hunters and spread swiftly through Asia, Africa and America. Their success was probably due to the hunting techniques of the dogs. Most modern dogs hunt in packs, and prehistoric dogs probably hunted in a similar way. Each pack has a leader. When a hunt begins the leader selects the prey animal and organizes the movements of the other dogs. If one dog tires, another takes over the chase. Because the dogs act together they have a better chance of catching their prey.

The dog relatives

The dog family is one of the most widespread and varied groups of mammals. True dogs include wolves, jackals and hyenas, as well as the domestic dog. Bears (below), racoons, seals, walruses and otters (right) are also distantly related to the dogs. Members of the dog family live wild on every continent and are among the world's most successful predators.

Primates

The history of the primates is important, as humans are a part of this group. When they study ancient primates, scientists are dealing with our own ancestors.

The very earliest primate fossils are of a creature known as *Purgatorius*. This small animal lived at the same time as dinosaurs such as *Tyrannosaurus* and *Triceratops*. Since only a few fossilized teeth and pieces of jaw have been found, we do not know very much about this animal.

Scientists know much more about *Plesiadapis,* which lived about 60 million years ago in Europe. This creature was nearly 70 cm (27 in) long and lived in tree tops where it ate leaves and fruits. *Plesiadapis* probably looked more like a squirrel than a monkey.

Over the following ten million years the primates gradually became better suited to life in the trees. The thumb became positioned so that it could push against the fingers to grasp a branch more securely. The eyes moved to the front of the head. In this position they were more useful for judging distances from one branch to the next. The primates also developed larger brains. Perhaps these also helped them to judge distances when leaping around in trees.

By about 40 million years ago the three main modern groups of primates had appeared. These are the New World monkeys, the Old World monkeys and the apes.

The primates are very adaptable. The ring-tailed lemur (above right) lives in trees while the gorilla (above left) lives on the floor of dense African jungles.

Perhaps the earliest known ape was *Aegyptopithecus*, which means "Egyptian ape." This creature lived in North Africa about 28 million years ago. It lived in the trees and had a short tail. *Aegyptopithecus* ate almost anything it could reach, including leaves, fruit, insects and small reptiles. Gibbons, gorillas and humans are probably descended from this creature.

Perhaps the oldest ancestor of the monkeys was *Notharctus*, which lived in America about 45 million years ago. This creature was rather similar to the lemurs, the primates which live on Madagascar. The lemurs have managed to survive to the present day, although they are among the most primitive mammals. They still retain all five fingers and toes on hands and feet and they have not changed in any special way.

Left: **Aegyptopith-ecus was one of the earliest apes.**

Australian Mammals

The mammals we have looked at so far in this book belong to many different families. They lived in widely scattered areas. However, there was one continent on which none of these animals lived. Instead a whole range of entirely different mammals has developed there. This area is Australia and the mammals are marsupials.

Throughout the age of mammals, Australia was cut off from the rest of the world by deep seas. Only creatures that could fly or swim, such as birds, insects and fish, were able to reach this continent. The vast numbers of cats, ruminants, elephants and other mammals could not make the crossing. The result was that Australia developed an animal life entirely unlike that of any other place on earth.

Most Australian mammals are marsupials. This group of mammals gives birth to its young at a very early stage. The baby then crawls into a furry pouch on its mother's stomach. It stays there suckling milk until it is big enough to look after itself. Some marsupials return to their mother's pouch even when they are several months old.

Above: **The kangaroo hops on its hind legs and can move very quickly. In some areas it is so common that it is regarded as a pest.**

Left: **The wombat is a slow-moving plant eater.**

Very few fossils of prehistoric marsupials have been found in Australia. Scientists cannot be certain how the different creatures are related to each other, nor how they evolved.

The most amazing marsupials in Australia are the kangaroos. Several species of these plant eaters exist. The largest is the red kangaroo which can measure well over 2 m (6.5 ft).

Kangaroos use their hind legs to jump at high speed. Some kangaroos can cover 10 m (33 ft) in a single bound and have been known to outrun a horse. Wombats are much smaller and dig long burrows under the ground. The koalas are probably the best known of the Australian marsupials. These small creatures move slowly through the trees eating eucalyptus leaves.

Marsupial predators have also evolved in Australia. The largest of these is the Tasmanian wolf, which is not related to wolves at all. This creature looks like a dog and lives by hunting kangaroos. It may now be extinct. Smaller hunters, such as the Tasmanian devil and the native cat, also evolved and fed on wombats and other marsupials.

Left: **The koala lives in eucalyptus trees and feeds on their leaves.**

Below: **The Tasmanian wolf was the largest meat-eating marsupial.**

Tasmanian wolf

Glossary

Ammonites A type of shellfish, related to squids. They were very common in prehistoric times.

Camouflage Markings on an animal's skin or fur that make it difficult to see the animal when it is hiding. A tiger's stripes help it to hide in the jungle, for example.

Climate The typical weather of an area. A desert has a hot, dry climate, for example.

Dinosaurs A group of very successful reptiles that dominated the earth for 150 million years. Dinosaurs died out about 65 million years ago.

Evolve To change and develop gradually, sometimes over millions of years.

Extinct Having died out. When every single specimen of a type of animal dies, the type is said to be extinct.

Fossils Remains of a plant or animal which have turned to stone.

Mammals One of several groups of animals. All mammals are warm blooded and produce milk to feed their young.

Marsupials One of the three main types of mammals. Marsupials care for their young in a pouch.

Placentals One of the three main types of mammals. Placentals give birth to fully formed young.

Plankton Tiny animals and plants which float in seas and lakes and can only be seen with a microscope.

Plesiosaurs Prehistoric reptiles which lived in the seas. They had long necks and limbs like paddles.

Predators Creatures that live by hunting and killing other animals.

Primates The group of mammals that includes humans, apes and monkeys.

Prototherians One of the three main types of mammals. Prototherians lay eggs.

Pterodactyls Prehistoric flying reptiles.

Regurgitates Brings partly-digested food back up to the mouth.

Reptiles Creatures with scaly skins and cold blood that lay eggs. All dinosaurs were reptiles. Examples of modern reptiles are snakes, lizards and crocodiles.

Rumen The first part of the stomach in some animals, such as cows. Food is partly digested here before being brought back into the mouth and chewed up again.

Ungulates Mammals with hoofs, such as horses, cattle and pigs.

Books to read

Benton, Michael, **The Story of Life on Earth**.
(Franklin Watts, 1986).

Cooke, Jean, **Archaeology**, Updated Edition.
(Warwick, 1982).

Curtis, Neil, **Fossils**. (Franklin Watts, 1984).

Gallant, Roy A., **Fossils**. (Franklin Watts, 1985).

Gallant, Roy A., **The Rise of Mammals**.
(Franklin Watts, 1986).

Lampton, Christopher, **Mass Extinctions: One Theory of Why the Dinosaurs Vanished**. (Franklin Watts, 1986).

Penny, Malcolm, **Animal Evolution**.
(Bookwright, 1987).

Strachan, Elizabeth, **A Closer Look at Prehistoric Mammals**, Rev. Edn.
(Gloucester, 1985).

Picture acknowledgments

The photographs in this book were supplied by: Bruce Coleman Ltd:
John Shaw 4 (top), Hans Reinhard 4 (bottom), 18, Gunter Ziesler 23, Lee
Lyon 26 (left), C.B. & D.W. Frith 28 (bottom); Geoscience Features Picture
Library 15; Oxford Scientific Films: Kathie Atkinson 7, Stouffer Productions 25
(top), Tom Ulrich 25 (bottom left), J.A.L. Cooke 28 (top), Alan G. Nelson 29.

Index

DATE DUE			
MAY 3 1992			
DEC. 8 1992			
OCT. 04 1993			
OCT. 1995			
FEB 10 '97			